OUTSTANDING AFRICAN AMERICANS

GREAT AFRICAN AMERICANS IN

Music

PAT REDIGER

Crabtree Publishing Company

Dedication

This series is dedicated to the African-American men and women who dared to follow their dreams. With courage, faith, and hard work, they overcame obstacles in their lives and went on to excel in their fields. They fought for civil rights and encouraged hope and self-reliance. They celebrated the glory of the athlete and the joy of knowledge and learning. They brought entertainment, poetry, and song to the world, and we are richer for it. *Outstanding African Americans* is both an acknowledgement of and a tribute to these people.

Project Manager
Amanda Woodrow

Writing Team
Karen Dudley
Pat Rediger

Editor
Virginia Mainprize

Research
Karen Dudley

Design and layout
Warren Clark
Karen Dudley

Photograph Credits

Archive Photos: pages 11, 19 (Frank Driggs Collection), 23, 24, 36, 40, 46, 49, 52, 55, 58, 61; **UPI/Bettman:** pages 7, 14, 15, 16, 17, 34, 42; **Blackstar:** pages 20 (Friedman), 26 (Quinones), 33 (Harrington), 38 (Partridge), 45 (Redfern); **Canapress Photo Service:** pages 5, 21, 37, 41; **Globe Photos:** pages 4, 9, 10, 13, 25, 27, 31, 32, 35, 43, 49, 55; **Ponopresse Internationale Inc.:** pages 12, 22, 30, 39, 44; **Retna Ltd.:** pages 8 (Stoll), 28 (Rider), 29 (Benabib); **Schomburg Center for Research in Black Culture, The New York Public Library, Astor, Lenox and Tilden Foundations:** pages 6, 18.

Published by
Crabtree Publishing Company

350 Fifth Avenue,	360 York Road, R.R. 4	73 Lime Walk
Suite 3308	Niagara-on-the-Lake,	Headington
New York, New York	Ontario Canada	Oxford Ox3 7AD
U.S.A. 10018	L0S 1J0	United Kingdom

Cataloging-in-Publication Data

Rediger, Pat. 1966-
    Great African Americans in music/by Pat Rediger.
        p. cm.—(Outstanding African Americans series)
    Includes index.
    Summay: Profiles notable African Americans in the field of music, including Ray Charles, Nat King Cole, and Ella Fitzgerald.
    ISBN 0-86505-800-8 (lib. bdg.) — ISBN 56505-814-8 (pbk.)
    1. Afro-American musicians Diography—Juvenile literature. [1. Musicians. 2. Afro Americans—Biography.] I. Title. II. Series: Rediger, Pat, 1966- Outstanding African Americans series.
ML3929.R43 1995   95-30397
780'.92'273—dc20   CIP
[B]   AC MN

Contents

Ray Charles

Personality Profile

Career: Singer, pianist, and songwriter.

Born: September 23, 1930, in Albany, Georgia, to Bailey and Aretha Robinson.

Family: Married Bernice Rosengarden, 1940, (divorced); married Della, 1954. Has three sons, Ray, Jr., David, and Robert.

Education: St. Augustine School for Deaf and Blind Children.

Awards: New Star Award, top male vocalist, *Down Beat*, 1961-65; No. 1 Male Singer, International Jazz Critics Poll, 1968; eleven Grammy awards; *Playboy* Jazz & Pop Hall of Fame; Songwriters Hall of Fame; Honorary Life Chairman, Rhythm & Blues Hall of Fame; *Ebony* Black Music Hall of Fame; NAACP Hall of Fame Award, 1983; B'nai B'rith Man of the Year; Rock and Roll Hall of Fame, Kennedy Center Honors Medal, 1986; Lifetime Achievement Award, National Academy of Recording Arts and Sciences, 1988.

Growing Up

Whenever Ray goes on tour, he attracts huge audiences.

Ray grew up in Greenville, Florida, where he was raised by his mother. His father was a railroad repairman who was often away from home, so Ray hardly saw him. Ray's mother took in laundry for a living, and the family struggled to make ends meet.

As Ray says about himself, he was born with music inside him. In 1933, by the time he was three, he had taught himself to play the piano. He spent a lot of time at the local Red Wing Café, listening to blues and big-band records on the juke box and to the owner playing the piano. Soon he was playing blues and boogie woogie himself.

When he was five, Ray's sight began to get blurred, and by the time he was seven, he was totally blind. He was sent to the St. Augustine School for Deaf and Blind Children where he learned to compose music in braille, a writing system for blind people. Ray also learned to play the clarinet, saxophone, organ, and trumpet.

Ray enjoyed the gospel music at the local Baptist church, and he listened to country music on the radio station. He especially enjoyed "The Grand Ole Opry," a radio program which featured country-music stars every Saturday night.

Developing Skills

"I guess what I'm trying to say is that I've loved any kind of music, as long as it was good."

R ay's mother died suddenly of food poisoning in 1945, when he was fifteen. Ray never returned to school after her funeral, and when his father died shortly after from diabetes, Ray decided to leave Greenville and support himself as a musician.

He headed off to nearby Jacksonville where he stayed with family friends and got a few jobs playing the piano with local bands. The next year, in 1946, Ray moved to Orlando, Florida, hoping to find more work. Here he was entirely on his own and found himself competing for jobs with many other musicians. Barely able to survive on his earnings, Ray decided to try his luck in Tampa, Florida. He landed a job with the Florida Playboys, an all-white country-and-western band.

Ray performing during a recording session.

At age seventeen, Ray got restless and boarded a bus to Seattle, Washington. The day after he arrived, he won a talent contest at a club called the Rocking Chair and was offered a steady job as a musician. Ray and the other club musicians formed a band called the McSon Trio, and soon they were playing all over Seattle. In 1948, they released their first single, "Confession Blues."

In 1950, Ray and his band moved to Los Angeles, California, where they recorded with Swingtime Records. Ray's first big hit was a rhythm-and-blues song he had written, "Baby, Let Me Hold Your Hand." It was a hit among African Americans, and by 1953, it had sold over 100,000 copies.

Ray joined Lowell Fulsom's blues band, but he continued to record his own songs. Atlantic Records, a small rhythm-and-blues company in New York City, liked Ray's music and bought his contract from Swingtime. Ray began to live on the road, touring black beer halls and night clubs and usually playing with local musicians. After a while, he grew frustrated with these musicians, many of whom were third-rate. Finally, in 1954, Ray formed his own seven-piece band and began experimenting with new musical styles.

In 1981, Ray became the 1,740th star to be honored on the Hollywood Walk of Fame.

In 1959, at twenty-nine, Ray recorded "What'd I Say." It was a smash hit among both black and white audiences and sold more than a million copies. His popularity grew, and Ray produced many more albums and began touring around the world, attracting huge audiences wherever he went. In 1965, Ray formed his own record company, Tangerine, and later changed its name to Crossover.

Accomplishments

1948	Formed the McSon Trio; signed with Swingtime Records.
1950	Released first hit, "Baby, Let Me Hold Your Hand."
1952	Signed with Atlantic Records.
1954	Formed his own band; first major hit, "I Got a Woman."
1959	"What'd I Say" sold over one million copies; signed with ABC-Paramount.
1961	Released *Genius + Soul = Jazz.*
1965	Formed his own record company, Tangerine.
1972	Released *A Message from the People.*
1990	Released *Would You Believe?*

Overcoming Obstacles

Although his family had very little money, the first years of Ray's childhood were happy. But everything changed after his younger brother, George, fell into a large washtub in the yard and drowned. Ray, only five years old at the time, tried to lift him out of the tub, but George was too heavy. By the time Ray got his mother, it was too late.

Shortly after his brother's death, Ray started waking up each morning with watery eyes. His vision began to blur, and within two years, he was completely blind. Ray's mother was determined that he live a normal life. She encouraged him to keep playing with the neighborhood children and continued to give him household chores to complete.

When Ray's parents died, he was left with nothing. He knew that if he stayed in Greenville, he would have to live on charity – something his mother would have hated. So Ray headed off to become a musician.

It was difficult at first as Ray competed with other musicians for work. Ray often lost jobs to them. At times, he lived on only crackers and sardines.

When Ray began touring with Lowell Fulsom's band, the audiences said that Ray sang like Nat King Cole. Ray welcomed the praise, but he wanted to be known for his own music.

Ray began to experiment with his singing, recording his own songs, and developing his own distinctive sound. Fortunately, Atlantic Records liked Ray's music and encouraged him to try new songs. In 1954, Ray recorded "I Got a Woman," a traditional gospel tune to which he had rewritten the lyrics. It was the first recording in a style which was later called "soul music." The song was an international hit, and Ray rose to stardom.

Over the next few years, some people criticized Ray's music because it combined blues with gospel. They felt that gospel was religious music and should be sung only in churches. But Ray was too busy creating his own music to pay much attention to his critics. By 1961, he was named one of the top, male, American vocalists.

Over the next thirty years, Ray continued to experiment with music, winning eleven Grammy awards in the process. Although he is now in his mid-sixties, Ray says that he will never retire.

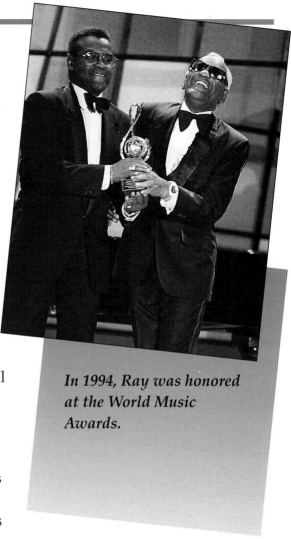

In 1994, Ray was honored at the World Music Awards.

Special Interests

- Ray has helped people with hearing problems. He formed the Robinson Foundation for Hearing Disorders. Ray gave the foundation $1 million.
- Ray has been a spokesperson for the civil rights movement. He received a NAACP Hall of Fame Award in 1983.
- Ray learned to play chess while recovering from drug abuse. It is now his favorite game.

Nat King Cole

Personality Profile

Career: Singer, songwriter, and pianist.

Born: March 17, 1919, in Montgomery, Alabama, to Edward and Perlina Coles.

Died: February 15, 1965, in Santa Monica, California.

Family: Married Nadine Robinson, 1937, (divorced, 1946); married Maria Ellington, 1948. Had two daughters, Stephanie Natalie Maria, and Carol.

Education: Wendell Phillips High School.

Awards: Winner of numerous awards including: popularity polls conducted by *Down Beat, Metronome, Esquire,* and *Billboard;* Recognition Award, Catholic War Veterans, 1955; Lifetime Achievement Award, National Academy of Recording Arts and Sciences, 1990; U.S. stamp issued in his honor, 1994.

Growing Up

Nat was born in Montgomery, Alabama, in 1919. He was raised in Chicago, Illinois, where his father was pastor in the True Light Baptist Church. All the Coles children were taught music by their mother who was the director of the church choir. When Nat was four years old, he could pick out tunes on the piano. The first song he played was "Yes, We Have No Bananas." By the time Nat was twelve, he was playing the organ at his father's church.

Until that time, Nat had been playing the piano by ear. But when he was twelve, his mother, Perlina, decided that Nat should take lessons in classical music. For the next six years, Nat played "everything from Bach to Rachmaninoff."

Nat was born Nat Coles, but he later dropped the "s" from his last name.

Despite his classical training, Nat was drawn to jazz. While in high school, he started his own band, and Perlina made the boys matching shirts so they would look like professional musicians. The band did not make much money – only $1.50 for an evening's performance. Sometimes all they got were free hamburgers and hot dogs.

But Nat was hooked on jazz, and when he graduated from high school in 1936 at age seventeen, he became the pianist for the black musical *Shuffle Along*.

W hen *Shuffle Along* traveled to Los Angeles, California, Nat went with the show. But when the musical closed, he was stranded. He managed to earn a little money playing in small night clubs and bars until a club manager asked him to form his own band and play at his club. As a publicity stunt, the manager called him King Cole, and soon the band was known as the King Cole Trio.

Nat's first band was known as the King Cole Trio.

For a while, the band had no singer, and Nat only played the piano. But he was becoming more interested in singing and, in 1937, got his chance as a vocalist when a customer requested the song "Sweet Lorraine." The audience loved Nat's warm, husky voice, and he began his singing career.

In 1943, Nat and the trio recorded their first hit, "Straighten Up and Fly Right," which sold a million copies and gained Nat millions of fans. Other recordings soon followed. In 1946, the King Cole Trio appeared on the "Kraft Music Hall" radio show. They were the summer replacements for the famous singer Bing Crosby. They also appeared in four musical motion pictures and received $13,500 for two days of work.

As Nat became more interested in singing, the band began to stress Nat's voice rather than the instruments. It was a smart move. Nat was soon in great demand, and the band toured across the country. In 1950, Nat went on his first tour of Europe where he made many new fans.

In 1956, Nat became the first African American to host a television show. It was called "The Nat King Cole Show" and lasted about a year. Nat appeared in movies such as *The Nat King Cole Story* and *Cat Ballou*. He also produced a musical play in 1960 called *I'm with You*.

Throughout the late 1950s and early 1960s, Nat's popularity grew. He sang at Carnegie Hall and performed for President Kennedy. But Nat's career was cut short in 1964 when he was diagnosed with lung cancer. He died on February 15, 1965, at the height of his career. He was forty-five years old.

In 1960, Nat met Queen Elizabeth II after performing in a Royal Variety Show in London, England.

Accomplishments

1936 Joined the musical *Shuffle Along*.	**1955** Starred in the movie *The Nat King Cole Story*.
1937 Formed the King Cole Trio.	**1956** Hosted the television show "The Nat King Cole Show."
1943 First hit song, "Straighten Up and Fly Away."	**1963** Last million-selling album, *Those Crazy Lazy Hazy Days of Summer*.
1948 Released song "Nature Boy."	
1950 First European tour.	

Overcoming Obstacles

Nat's early days in the music industry were tough. It was hard earning a living in small night clubs, and when Nat formed his own band, a club owner insisted that he wear a gold paper crown. He told Nat his new name was King Cole. Nat did not want to wear the crown, but he had little choice. He needed the job. After a few weeks, Nat managed to get rid of the crown, but the name stuck.

After a few months of just playing the piano for the band, Nat started to get a little bored. He began to sing occasionally but believed that he had a terrible voice. However, the audiences loved his singing style and his voice which was described as glowing and hip. Soon he became known as a singer who plays the piano rather than just a piano player.

Despite all his success, Nat faced racism. In 1948, some neighbors protested when he moved into an area where only white people lived. They hired a lawyer who told Nat that undesirable people were not welcome in the neighborhood. He was actually talking about Nat, but Nat pretended not to understand. He told the lawyer that if he saw any undesirable people coming, he would be the first to complain.

"If you think about it, ninety percent of the popular stars today, including myself, have no voice, but they have soul, that appeal that will touch the average guy."

Nat broke other racial barriers. He sued hotels for not letting him stay in their rooms, and he performed at segregated clubs that had not let blacks in before.

But Nat could succeed only so far in the fight against racism. Although his television show had good ratings, he could not find a permanent sponsor because the big advertisers did not want to take a chance. They felt that whites might not watch a program featuring an African American, and that it would be a waste of money to advertise on the show. As a result, the show lasted only a year.

On April 11, 1956, Nat experienced a violent form of racism when he was attacked by six white men during a performance in Birmingham, Alabama. Although Nat suffered a back injury, his attackers received only minor punishments.

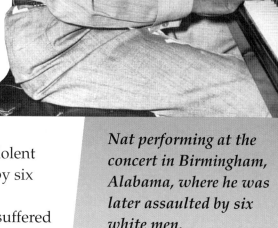

Nat performing at the concert in Birmingham, Alabama, where he was later assaulted by six white men.

Special Interests

- Nat's hobbies were photography and collecting records of his favorite music and singers.
- Nat was interested in helping war veterans. He entertained patients at veterans' hospitals across the country.
- Nat was active in the civil rights movement. He was a member of the National Association for the Advancement of Colored People (NAACP).

Ella Fitzgerald

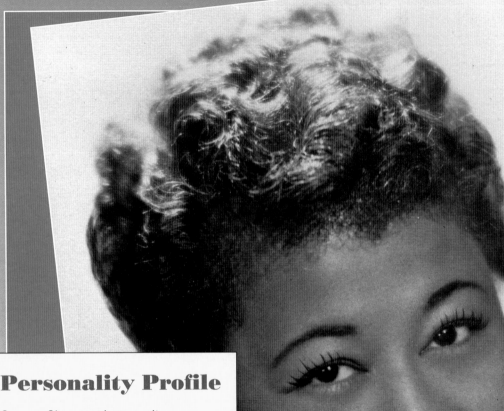

Personality Profile

Career: Singer and songwriter.

Born: April 25, 1917, in Newport News City, Virginia, to William and Tempie Fitzgerald.

Education: Benjamin Franklin Junior High School.

Family: Married Benny Kornegay, 1941, (marriage annulled soon after); married Ray Brown, 1947, (divorced, 1953). Has an adopted son, Ray, Jr.

Awards: Winner of numerous awards including: thirteen Grammy awards; Bing Crosby Award, 1967; named top female singer at the 16th International Jazz Critics Poll, 1968; American Music Award, 1978; Kennedy Center Honor, 1979; Woman of the Year, Harvard's Hasty Pudding Club, 1982: honorary degree from Howard University, 1985; Honorary Doctor of Music, Yale University, 1987; National Medal of the Arts presented at the White House, 1987; Society of Singers Lifetime Achievement Award, 1989.

Growing Up

Ella was born in Newport News City, Virginia, in 1917. A year after she was born, her father abandoned the family. Ella's mother, Tempie, and the new man in her life moved to Yonkers, New York, taking baby Ella with them. They moved into a neighborhood of Italians and African Americans where Ella spent a happy childhood.

Music and song were always a part of Ella's life. Radio and records, which were new then, brought music into her home. When Ella was in the third grade, she began to dance. She and her friends practiced dance steps in the street and put on shows for their friends. Ella also loved to sing, and she got her first training at the local Baptist church choir. She had a gift for imitation and could copy any singing style. She also had relative pitch which allowed her to sing each note perfectly in tune. Soon she was singing jazz, the popular music of the day, imitating the great jazz singers she heard on the radio.

"I wanted to do something, I wanted to make something of myself."

At first Ella wanted to be a dancer. When she was a teenager, she used to sneak off to the Savoy Ballroom in Harlem to learn the latest dance stops. Soon she was getting dance jobs in clubs.

In 1932, when Ella was fifteen, her mother died suddenly of a heart attack. The next few years were very difficult for Ella. She moved in with an aunt and dropped out of school. She hung around an area known as Black Broadway where dancers, jugglers, and singers performed on the street. Soon Ella was living on the street with these people.

Developing Skills

One day, Ella's friends suggested she enter a talent contest at the Apollo Theater in Harlem. She arrived at the club wearing cast-off clothing and men's boots because she couldn't afford anything else. She hadn't had a bath for many weeks. She was planning to dance but, at the last minute, decided to sing instead. At first her voice cracked, but by the end of her song she had brought the house down. She won first prize which included the promise of a week's work at the theater. However, Ella was never given her prize. The Apollo thought she looked too dirty and untidy to appear on stage. So Ella returned to live on the street.

Chick Webb, one of the best-known jazz musicians, heard about Ella and offered her a job as a singer with his band. Ella joined the band and began singing at the famous Savoy Ballroom. She threw herself into her new role as a jazz singer. She memorized the words to songs amazingly quickly and could learn the tunes just as fast. Ella was seventeen years old.

Within a few weeks, Ella recorded "Love and Kisses." Her singing skills improved, and two years later she was voted Number One Female Vocalist by *Melody* magazine. In 1938, she wrote and recorded her famous jazz version of the nursery rhyme "A-Tisket A-Tasket." It became an instant success and is still one of her most famous songs.

Sometimes Ella teamed up with other great singers such as Nat King Cole.

Chick's sudden death in 1939 was a great loss to Ella and the jazz world. She took over as leader of the band which became Ella Fitzgerald and her Famous Orchestra. The band toured all across the country, but after three years, it broke up. Ella began performing on her own.

Ella continued to develop her unique singing style and soon became an international star, performing in concert halls all over the world and recording many albums. She has appeared on many television shows and has performed at the top jazz festivals. She sang at the gala ball to celebrate President Kennedy's inauguration. Today, she is considered one of the greatest jazz musicians of all time.

Ella performing at the famous Savoy Ballroom in New York.

Accomplishments

1934 Won first place on amateur night at the Harlem Opera House. Won talent competition at the Apollo Theater.

1935 Became a professional singer with Chick Webb's band; recorded first record, "Love and Kisses."

1936 Made famous recording "If You Can't Sing It, You'll Have to Swing It."

1938 Wrote and recorded "A-Tisket, A-Tasket."

1944 Recorded "Into Each Life Some Rain Must Fall."

1958 Released *Gershwin Songbook.*

1960 Released *Mack the Knife.*

1963 Released *These Are the Blues.*

1966 Released "These Boots Are Made for Walkin'" and "Sweet Georgia Brown."

1973 Released *Take Love Easy* .

1974 Released *Ella in London.*

1979 Released *A Perfect Match: Ella & Basie.*

Overcoming Obstacles

When Chick Webb was looking for a singer for his band, someone suggested Ella to him. At first, he didn't want to listen to her. She was awkward and shy and had no experience. Because she had been living on the streets, she wore dirty clothes and had not had a bath for many weeks. She didn't look like someone who could perform in public. Finally he agreed to give her a chance.

In 1990, Ella received an honorary doctorate in Music from Harvard University.

Ella's singing impressed Chick, and he agreed to add her to his band. At first, the band members teased Ella about her appearance. The lead trombone player told her to go and wash with soap and water, but she still sang in her street clothes because that was all she had. She wasn't paid a regular salary, and Chick gave her a few dollars now and then.

Within a few weeks, Chick realized what an incredible voice Ella had and asked her to sign a contract. Ella began to become more confident, and her audiences loved her. In 1938, Ella recorded "A-Tisket A Tasket" which sold a million copies in a few weeks and rocketed her to fame.

When Chick died the following year, Ella and the band were on tour. They hadn't read the newspaper that day and went on stage to perform. At the end of the song, no one in the audience applauded. Only then did the band discover that Chick was dead. Ella was stricken with grief, but she realized she would have to continue because the band needed her. Although she was only twenty-one, she became the band leader.

Ella with Quincy Jones, Bobby McFerrin, and Lena Horne at a 1990 benefit performance.

Over the years, success followed success. Of Ella's over two hundred recordings, thirteen have won Grammy awards. Again and again, Ella has been voted the most popular jazz singer. In 1993, Ella appeared on stage for the last time at New York's Carnegie Hall.

Special Interests

- Until her mid-seventies, Ella kept busy working about forty weeks a year.
- Ella supports various community organizations. In 1990, she gave a benefit concert in New York for the American Heart Association.
- Ella always loved children. She first became involved in helping orphaned and disadvantaged children in 1947. In 1977, The Ella Fitzgerald Child Care Center was opened in Watts, Los Angeles.

Aretha Franklin

Personality Profile

Career: Singer.

Born: March 25, 1942, in Memphis, Tennessee, to Clarence and Barbara Franklin.

Education: Northern High School, Detroit.

Family: Married Ted White, 1961, (divorced 1969); married Glynn Turman, 1978, (divorced 1984). Has four sons, Clarence, Edward, Teddy, Jr., and Kecalf.

Awards: Fifteen Grammy awards; three American Music Awards; named Top Female Vocalist by *Billboard, Cashbox,* and *Record World* magazines, 1967; City of Detroit declares Aretha Franklin Day on February 16, 1968; inducted into Rock and Roll Hall of Fame, 1987; Lifetime Achievement Award, National Academy of Recording Arts and Sciences, 1994; Kennedy Center Honor, 1994.

Growing Up

Aretha grew up with music. Her mother was a popular gospel singer, and her father, the minister of a Baptist church in Detroit, was a well-known preacher and singer. Many famous singers and musicians visited the Franklin household and enouraged Aretha to sing. She learned to play the piano as a child, and she and her sisters would sometimes spend the whole day singing.

In 1948, when Aretha was six, her mother left the family. The housekeepers who looked after the children when their father was traveling on preaching and singing tours never filled the space left by Aretha's mother.

When Aretha's aunt died, Clara Ward, a famous gospel singer, performed at the funeral. Aretha was so enchanted with Clara's singing that she decided to become a singer. She performed her first solo in her father's church when she was twelve years old. At fourteen, Aretha began traveling and singing with her father when he preached in other churches. That same year, 1956, she made her first recording of gospel music and soon became a famous, teenage gospel singer.

"There was always music in our house. The radio was going in one room, the record player in another, the piano banging away in the living room."

Developing Skills

I n 1960, Aretha decided to try a career as a blues singer. Her father supported her decision, and she left Detroit for New York City in search of stardom.

After years of singing gospel music, Aretha decided to try singing blues.

Aretha sent a recording of her music to John Hammond, a music producer with Columbia Records. John was entranced with her singing and said that hers was the best voice he had heard in twenty years. He offered her a five-year contract and became her producer. Two years later, *Down Beat* magazine named Aretha the top new star in jazz. She sang in clubs and made several albums.

After her contract with Columbia ended, Aretha signed with Atlantic Records who gave her the freedom to choose her own music. They also encouraged her to make use of new recording technology. When recording a song, she first sang and played the piano. Then she would sing as one of the back-up voices. Finally, the remaining voices and instruments were taped, and the three recordings were blended together. The results sent Aretha to the top of the charts.

Aretha was fortunate to be singing at a time when whites were becoming interested in black musicians. For years, whites purchased only recordings made by white musicians. Times were changing, and Aretha's music and style appealed to all audiences.

Aretha has sold millions of records around the world, and she has received many awards. She has produced twenty-four gold (or best-selling) albums in twenty years. Aretha remains one of the country's top performers and one of the world's greatest living singers. In 1987, she became the first woman to be inducted into the Rock and Roll Hall of Fame. She has also won fifteen Grammy awards – more than any other woman performer. She is currently working on her autobiography and a new album.

In 1986, the state of Michigan declared Aretha's voice to be one of its natural resources.

Accomplishments

1960 Signed a five-year contract with Columbia Records.

1961 Released first album, *Aretha.*

1965 Signed with Atlantic Records.

1967 Released "Respect," "Chain of Fools," and "Dr. Feelgood."

1972 Released "Amazing Grace" and "Young, Gifted, and Black."

1985 Released "Who's Zoomin Who."

1989 Released "Through the Storm."

Overcoming Obstacles

T raveling as a singer with her father when he preached at other churches, Aretha spent much of her teenage years on the road. It was a difficult life; she dropped out of school, and she missed her friends in Detroit. When she traveled in the South, she experienced white racism for the first time. She and her father often were forced to eat in the blacks-only section of restaurants.

"Sometimes I still have a problem [with stage fright]…all those people sitting out there looking at me….I've overcome it just by walking out onstage night after night, year after year."

In 1957, when Aretha was fifteen, she became pregnant. She named her son Clarence Franklin after her father. Her grandmother and sister helped look after Aretha's son so she could continue her singing career. This was a sad time in Aretha's life, and she became interested in blues music because it reflected the way she was feeling.

Aretha started to plan her career as a musician. She knew she wanted to be a blues singer. But Aretha was worried that her father might not approve because he had spent years teaching her how to sing gospel music. Fortunately, he understood and gave her his blessing to go to New York City to pursue her dream.

Two years after signing the contract with Columbia Records, Aretha was beginning to get frustrated. She did not like the pop songs Columbia wanted her to sing, and she was unhappy with the large orchestras which played the music. She wanted only a few instruments to accompany her. In addition, the company often booked her into second-rate night clubs. Because the contract lasted five years, Aretha had to do what Columbia wanted. But when the contract ended, she looked for a company that would allow her the freedom to explore blues music. She signed with Atlantic Records which encouraged her to choose her own material and develop her own style. It was the right decision.

Throughout her career, Aretha has won many awards including fifteen Grammies and three American Music Awards.

Aretha has suffered many personal tragedies. In 1979, her beloved father was shot by a burglar and stayed in a coma for five years. Aretha gave two benefit concerts to pay for his hospital costs. She was with him when he died in 1984. Her sister, Carolyn, who trained Aretha's back-up singers, died of cancer in 1988. Her brother, Cecil, who was her manager, died suddenly of a heart attack in 1990. These losses affected Aretha, but she feels they gave her singing more feeling. Now when Aretha sings "soul" music, it comes from the heart.

Special Interests

- Aretha donates much of her time and talent to charity. She has put on concerts to raise money for churches and community organizations. She also donates money to the United Negro College Fund and the National Association for the Advancement of Colored People (NAACP).
- In 1988, Aretha made a commercial against drinking and driving. The commercial changed the words to her song "Think" to "Think...Don't Drive with Drugs or Drink!"

Hammer

Personality Profile

Career: Rap singer, dancer, songwriter, and businessman.

Born: March 30, 1962, in Oakland, California, to Lewis Burrell.

Education: McClymonds High School.

Family: Married Stephanie. Has two children, Akeiba Monique and Sarah Brooke.

Awards: Five American Music Awards, 1991; People's Choice Award, 1991; three Grammy awards, 1991; named Booster of the Year by the Oakland Chamber of Commerce, 1991.

Growing Up

Hammer was born Stanley Kirk Burrell in Oakland, California, in 1962. He was the youngest of six children, and the entire family lived in a three-bedroom apartment. Money was pretty tight, and sometimes his parents had to take welfare when they could not find work. Hammer and his four brothers did odd jobs to help support the family.

By age three, Hammer was performing singing and dancing routines for his family. When he saw the famous soul and gospel singer James Brown on television, he began to imitate him. Hammer also took part in talent shows at his elementary school. But his first love was baseball.

One day, when Hammer was eleven, he sang and danced in the parking lot of the Oakland Coliseum, the home of the Oakland A's baseball team. The A's owner, Charlie Finley, spotted Hammer and was impressed with the boy's energy. Charlie asked Hammer to become an errand boy, and soon Hammer became the A's batboy. The players called him Little Hammer because he looked just like home-run champion, Hammerin' Hank Aaron. Hammer received a salary of $7.50 before each game and traveled with the club.

"I been dancing ever since I was born."

Developing Skills

After graduating from high school, Hammer went to a local community college while preparing to be a professional baseball player. He tried out for the San Francisco Giants but failed to make the team. Disappointed and uncertain about his future, Hammer joined the navy and served for three years.

When he left the navy in the early 1980s, Hammer became a devout Christian. He improved his singing and dancing and began performing gospel rap in Oakland clubs.

Hammer developed a popular stage show which he took on a world tour .

In 1987, at twenty-four, Hammer formed Bust It Records with a loan he received from two A's baseball players, Dwayne Murphy and Mike Davis. Hammer's first song was "Ring 'Em" which he sold out of the trunk of his car. Hammer also formed his own rap group which included two disc jockeys, three female singers, and a bodyguard.

That same year, Hammer began working on songs for his first album. He hired a professional music producer, and they put together *Feel My Power* in a makeshift studio in a basement apartment. Hammer's wife, Stephanie, helped promote the album by sending it to radio stations and night clubs that played taped music. Slowly, Hammer began to make a name for himself.

One night, a talent scout for Capitol Records saw Hammer's performance and immediately signed him to a contract. Hammer renamed his *Feel My Power* album to *Let's Get It Started*. It was a big success and sold more than 1.5 million copies. Hammer and his group went on tour, singing and dancing for enthusiastic audiences all over the United States.

In 1991, Hammer won three Grammy awards.

In 1989, Hammer recorded his second album in the back of his tour bus. It was called *Please Hammer Don't Hurt 'Em* and contained the huge hit "U Can't Touch This." The album sold more than ten million copies, making it the most successful rap album in history.

Hammer's third album was *Too Legit to Quit* which was released in 1991. Until this time, Hammer had used the initials M.C. before his name. M.C. is slang for rapper. Hammer dropped the initials because he was more than just an ordinary rapper.

Accomplishments

1987 Formed Bust It Records; produces first album, *Feel My Power*.

1988 Re-released *Feel My Power* as *Let's Get It Started*.

1989 Released *Please Hammer Don't Hurt 'Em*.

1990 First world tour.

1991 Released video for *Please Hammer Don't Hurt 'Em*. Released *Too Legit to Quit*.

1994 Released *The Funky Headhunter*; formed Roll Wit It Entertainment & Sports Management.

Overcoming Obstacles

When Hammer did not make the San Francisco Giants team, his future seemed unsure. He could have done what some people in his neighborhood were doing – sell drugs. Instead, he joined the navy. There he discovered the benefits of hard work and discipline. Later he used these techniques in training his singers and dancers.

Other rappers are Hammer's harshest critics. Rappers are street musicians who usually recite songs without backup music. Their songs are about the way they feel about life. Some rappers do not think Hammer is a good singer and do not like his use of backup singers and dancers.

Hammer feels his critics are just jealous of his success. He answers them by pointing out that he has introduced rap to a larger audience than any street rapper ever would.

In 1991, Hammer performed at a benefit concert for Kurdish refugees.

In recent years, some people have suggested Hammer was losing his popularity. When he sold his Bust It Records company and his race horse business to his family, some believed these were signs that Hammer was losing money. But that was not the case. In 1994, Hammer started a new business called Roll Wit It Entertainment & Sports Management which manages the careers of famous entertainers and sports personalities. Hammer also has released a new album, *The Funky Headhunter,* which was another big success. Hammer says he never lost his popularity; he just wanted to explore other interests.

Special Interests

- Hammer once owned nineteen race horses and several were champions. His race horse Lite Light won the 1991 Kentucky Oaks.
- Hammer runs five miles a day, dances for two-and-a-half hours, and then does 1,000 situps.
- Hammer enjoys collecting sports cars. They include a Porsche, a Mercedes-Benz, and a Ferrari.
- Today Hammer has more than two hundred people working for him. He tries to help people from his old neighborhood by hiring them to be part of his group.

Hammer and his group practice thirteen to fourteen hours a day, seven days a week.

Sarah Vaughan

Personality Profile

Career: Singer.

Born: March 27, 1924, in Newark, New Jersey, to Asbury and Ada Vaughan.

Died: April 4, 1990, in Hidden Hills, California.

Education: Arts High.

Family: Married George Treadwell, 1956, (divorced); married Clyde B. Atkins, 1959, (divorced); married Waymond Reed, 1978. Had an adopted daughter, Debra Lois.

Awards: Best female singer, *Down Beat*, 1947 to 1952; Best female singer, *Metronome,* 1948 to 1953; *Down Beat* International Jazz Critics Award, 1973, 1975 to 1979; Emmy award, 1981; Grammy award, 1982; received a star on the Hollywood Walk of Fame, 1985; inductee, Jazz Hall of Fame, 1988.

Growing Up

When Sarah was a child, her house was filled with music. Her mother, Ada, a talented singer and choir member in the local Baptist church, played the piano and taught Sarah how to sing. In the evenings, her father played country songs on his guitar. Every afternoon, Sarah ran home from school to listen to the radio or to play records.

In 1931, when Sarah was seven, she joined the church choir. She started taking piano lessons which cost twenty-five cents a week back then. By the time she was twelve, she was such a good player that she became the organist at her church.

Sarah's favorite music was jazz. She and her friends went to the local skating rink or to neighborhood dances featuring big jazz bands. She hung around record stores in downtown Newark, meeting musicians and listening to records. In those days, stores allowed people to listen to the music without buying the records.

"I thought I was just another little black girl for whom the future looked just as dark as it was for thousands of others like me."

In junior high, Sarah dropped out of school. She spent her days in the record store or at the Picadilly Club. She was only fifteen and under age, but the manager let her in to listen to the afternoon performances. Soon she started going there at night, playing the piano and earning a little money in tips. She also used to sneak into clubs and pool halls to listen to famous jazz musicians. Later, when Sarah was a successful singer, she performed with some of these musicians.

Developing Skills

I n 1942, when Sarah was eighteen, a friend dared her to enter an amateur contest at the Apollo Theater, a famous club in Harlem, New York. She arrived late and was so nervous she could barely tell the master of ceremonies what she wanted to do. He almost didn't let her on stage. But when Sarah sang "Body and Soul," the audience cheered. She won first prize of ten dollars and the chance to sing at the Apollo for a week.

Sarah's lovely voice and her ability to improvise helped her rise to fame.

Her chance came in the spring of 1943. Ella Fitzgerald was to be the featured singer, and the crowds came. Billy Eckstein, the famous jazz singer, arrived to listen to Ella and stayed for the whole show. When Sarah began to sing, he couldn't believe his ears. He told his bandleader, Earl "Fatha" Hines, about her. Earl heard Sarah sing and asked her to join his band. They performed at clubs in New York and toured across the country. Sarah was only nineteen years old.

Sarah had an amazing voice. She could sing any type of music, always keep in tune, and change keys with ease. As Dizzy Gillespie, who was playing with the Hines band when Sarah joined, said about her then, "Sarah can sing notes that other people can't even hear."

In 1944, Sarah decided to try her luck as a soloist, singing and playing the piano for whatever club jobs, out-of-town dates, and tours she could find.

Soon Sarah began to record her songs, and her popularity grew among musicians, and jazz music fans. In 1944, she released her first recording under her own name. In 1945, the song "Lover Man," which she performed with Dizzy Gillespie and Charlie Parker, became a hit. Today, Sarah's recordings from this period are all jazz classics.

As Sarah's popularity grew, she began to travel. She performed with all the great jazz musicians including Oscar Peterson and Count Basie. All over the world, her fans flocked to her concerts.

Ella Fitzgerald, one of the greatest jazz singers of all time, once said, "The greatest singing talent in the world today is Sarah Vaughan."

In 1985, Sarah received a star on the Hollywood Walk of Fame.

Accomplishments

1942	Won jazz contest at Apollo Theater in Harlem, New York.	**1953**	Embarked on first European tour.
1945	Released hit single "Lover Man."	**1985**	Received star on Hollywood Walk of Fame.
1946	Released hit single "Body and Soul."	**1990**	Inducted into Jazz Hall of Fame.

Overcoming Obstacles

Sarah performing at the Memphis Jazz Festival in 1957.

Sarah was determined to sing. Her father disapproved of Sarah's taste in music, but a career in classical music was not open to African Americans in those days. So Sarah became fascinated with jazz. In her late teens, she hung out at jazz clubs all night, listening to singers and musicians. She would sleep all day and then start all over again.

At first, the only money Sarah made was the tips people gave for her performance. When she joined Earl Hines's band, she did not have enough money even to get her dress cleaned. Later, she was paid fourteen dollars for every night the band performed, usually four nights a week. For her first recording she was paid only forty dollars.

New singers must sing in many locations. Early in Sarah's career, she often spent all year on the road, with only a night at each town and traveling thousands of miles by bus. Segregation laws in the South discriminated against blacks, and the band would often play a job and then find no place to eat or sleep. They could not always find black families who would rent out rooms, so they slept on the bus while the driver drove to the next job. Sometimes Sarah performed in well-known clubs, but she often played in tobacco warehouses and barns.

All her life, Sarah suffered from shyness. Even though she was in thousands of shows and sang in front of millions of people, she was always nervous before a performance. As she said, "I try to look relaxed onstage, but believe me, honey, it's only an act."

When Sarah died in 1990, a thousand people attended her funeral. Sarah's recording of "Ave Maria" was played, and a horse-drawn carriage took Sarah's coffin from the church to the graveyard. The world mourned the death of one of the greatest jazz singers of all time.

"I sing. I just sing."

Special Interests

- Sarah had several nicknames. Some called her "The Divine" while others called her "Sassy."
- Sarah loved to sew. She traveled with a sewing machine, and in her spare time, she would make herself dresses and gowns to wear during her performances.

Stevie Wonder

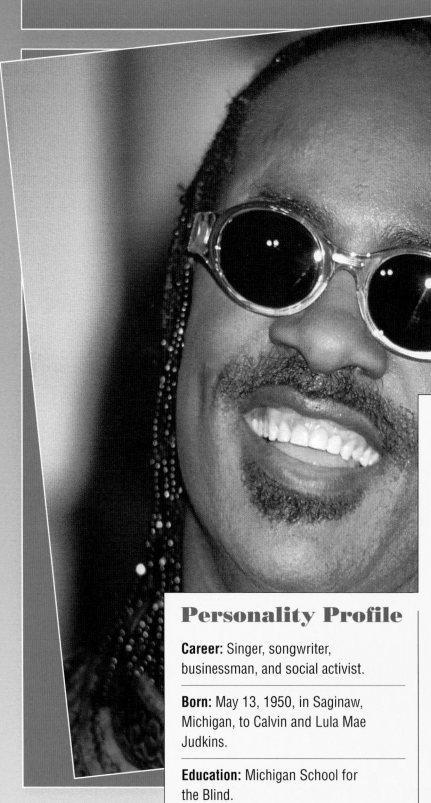

Family: Married Syreeta Wright, 197
(divorced, 1974). Has three children,
Aisha, Keita Sawandi, and Mumtaz
Ekow.

Awards: Seventeen Grammy awards
including Album of the Year 1973, 19
1976; American Music Award, 1978;
received numerous honors including
Show Business Inspiration Award;
Distinguished Service Award; B'nai
B'rith Man of the Year Award; Annua
Human Kindness Day Special Honore
American Video Award for Best Rhyt
and Blues Video for "Ebony & Ivory,"
1982; inducted into the Songwriters
of Fame, 1982; Academy Award for E
Original Song, "I Just Called to Say I
Love You," 1984; inducted into the R
and Roll Hall of Fame, 1989.

Personality Profile

Career: Singer, songwriter,
businessman, and social activist.

Born: May 13, 1950, in Saginaw,
Michigan, to Calvin and Lula Mae
Judkins.

Education: Michigan School for
the Blind.

Growing Up

When he was born, Stevie, who was named Stevland Judkins, was so tiny that the doctors placed him in an incubator. But something went wrong with the incubator, and Stevie went blind. Thanks to his two older brothers, Stevie enjoyed a happy childhood. They taught him to run and climb trees, and ride a bicycle if someone else steered.

By the time he was only two, Stevie showed a keen interest in music. He loved to listen to the radio and drum along with the music, using pots and pans and spoons. When he was four, he was playing the harmonica and the piano.

When Stevie was seven, his parents divorced, and he went to live with his mother who moved to Detroit, Michigan. He began to sing in the local church choir and became the soloist when he was nine. However, he was expelled from the choir because someone heard him singing rock and roll.

The next year, in 1960, a singer from Motown Records heard Stevie sing and introduced him to Berry Gordy, Jr., Motown's owner. Berry offered him a contract. For the next three years, Stevie spent all his free time at Motown's recording studios trying out the instruments, playing songs he had composed, and meeting Motown singers.

Stevie was only ten years old when he signed his first recording contract.

"I was always beating things like beating on tables with a spoon, or beating on those cardboard drums they used to give to kids."

Developing Skills

In 1963, Stevie made his first recording, "Fingertips Part 2," which featured him singing and playing the harmonica. Motown called him "Little Stevie Wonder," and the recording was a smash hit. It sold over one million copies and topped the record charts for fifteen weeks. Stevie became an instant star.

As a Motown singer, Stevie toured with other Motown musicians. A tutor went with him so he did not fall behind in his studies at the Michigan School for the Blind. During his teenage years, Stevie recorded an amazing number of hits, including "Uptight" and "I Was Made to Love Her."

Stevie plays a wide range of musical instruments including drums, synthesizers, and the harmonica.

In 1971, when he was twenty-one, Stevie broke away from Motown Records. Until then, Motown had controlled his money and the type of music he sang. Stevie wanted the freedom to record songs that expressed his feelings about civil rights for African Americans.

Stevie began experimenting with synthesizers, which allowed him to perform all parts of a song himself. He also learned about the business part of the recording industry.

The first album Stevie produced was *Music of My Mind*. By this time, Stevie and Berry had patched up their differences, and Motown agreed to promote and distribute the album. Stevie went on tour with The Rolling Stones, and people all over the country loved the new Stevie Wonder sound. The album was an incredible success.

When the tour finished, Stevie produced two more albums, *Talking Book* and *Innervisions*. *Talking Book* featured a number one hit, "Superstition," while *Innervisions* won a Grammy award.

Stevie has released many more best-selling albums since then. He has performed in England, Europe, Japan, and Africa. He has also appeared in movies and on television.

After a four-year absence, Stevie returned to the music scene in 1995 with the message of freedom and justice for all people. He toured the country and released a new album, *Conversation Peace*, with Branford Marsalis. After thirty years as a singer and musician, Stevie is as popular as ever.

In 1985, Stevie won an Academy Award for Best Song.

Accomplishments

1960 Signed a contract with Hitsville USA (later became Motown Records).

1963 Produced first hit single,"Fingertips Part 2."

1965 Produced hit single "Uptight."

1967 Produced hit single "I Was Made to Love Her."

1971 Established his own studio, production company, and publishing house.

1972 Produced *Music of My Mind;* tours with The Rolling Stones.

1976 Released *Songs in the Key of Life*, a triple album set.

1984 Released "I Just Called to Say I Love You" for the movie *The Woman in Red.*

Overcoming Obstacles

Blindness was Stevie's biggest obstacle, but it is one that he has overcome. He uses a reading machine which scans the printed words and then speaks them back to him. He also uses a computer that prints in braille, a writing system for blind people.

When Stevie was young, his mother could not afford to buy him musical instruments. Many friends and neighbors pitched in to help. His barber bought him a harmonica, the Lions Club gave him a set of drums for Christmas, and a neighbor who was moving gave him her piano.

Stevie with record producer Quincy Jones.

Although Motown started his career, after awhile Stevie was not happy with the company. He felt they had too much control over his money and the kind of music he played. He did not want to be called "Little Stevie Wonder" and tried to get Motown to change the name. Although Stevie did record some songs that he wanted, such as "Blowin' in the Wind" and "Mr. Tambourine Man," most of his songs were ones that Motown had chosen.

Stevie decided to leave Motown and set up his own studio. It was not an easy decision. Berry Gordy, Jr. was upset with Stevie, and for awhile the two men did not speak.

In August, 1973, Stevie was in a car accident. The accident made him rethink his goals in life, and he decided that he should become more than just an entertainer. He wanted to use his talent to make the world a better place. Stevie became involved in the civil rights movement and helped make Martin Luther King, Jr.'s birthday a national holiday.

Today Stevie works at improving the world by raising money for AIDS research and world hunger relief projects.

"The only people who are really blind are those...[who] can't see the light of love and justice."

Special Interests

- Stevie enjoys playing tennis. He uses a "beeping" tennis ball, so he knows where to hit it.
- Stevie is well-known for his television commercials against drinking and driving. He produced the song "Don't Drive Drunk" for these commercials.
- Stevie played a major role in the song "We Are the World." It was sung by Stevie and many other stars. Money from the song went to help starving people in Ethiopia, Africa.

Chuck Berry

Chuck wanted to be a musician, but he had to work in a factory to support his wife and children.

C huck, who is known as the father of rock and roll, started his musical career late in life. In 1939, when he was thirteen, he bought himself a six-string Spanish guitar and taught himself how to play. But before he finished high school, he was convicted of robbery and served three years in jail.

After he was released, Chuck wanted to be a musician, but he had to work in a factory to support his wife and children. He played the guitar part-time in an orchestra to earn extra money. In 1952, the pianist Johnnie Johnson asked Chuck to perform with him on New Year's Eve at the Cosmopolitan Club in St. Louis, Missouri. They were such a success that they performed there or at other black clubs for the next three years.

In 1955, Chuck met blues singer Muddy Waters who introduced him to Leonard Chess, president of Chess Records. Leonard was impressed and asked Chuck to record two songs he had written, "Maybelline" and "Wee Wee Hours." "Maybelline" became a rock-and-roll classic and an overnight success, and Chuck became a full-time musician. The next year he released "Roll Over Beethoven" and "Brown-Eyed Handsome Man." He also appeared in the movie *Rock, Rock, Rock*.

Throughout the 1950s, Chuck recorded many hit songs. One of his most famous was a song about himself called "Johnny B. Goode." It told the story of a rock star living and working in a big city.

When Chuck began to tour, he thrilled his audiences. They loved a special dance he performed called the duck walk in which he slinked across the stage with his knees bent.

When Chuck turned thirty-three, he began spending the money he had earned from his tours and records. He moved his family into a mansion in St. Louis, Missouri, and bought a fleet of Cadillacs. He began building Berry Park with a hotel, guitar-shaped swimming pool, golf course, and night club. But Chuck ran into trouble with the law, and he spent two years in prison. He used the time to finish his high school education and to write some of his best-known songs.

Personality Profile

Career: Singer, guitarist, and songwriter.

Born: January 15, 1926, in San José, California, to Henry and Martha Berry.

Education: Attended Sumner High School.

Awards: Best R&B Singer, Blues Unlimited 1973; Top Rock and Roll Entertainer, The Rock Music Awards, 1975; National Music Award, 1976; Grammy award for Lifetime Achievement, 1984; inducted into Rock and Roll Hall of Fame, 1986; Lifetime Achievement Award, *Guitar Player Magazine*, 1987; Hollywood Walk of Fame, 1987.

Chuck was released in 1964. He recorded two hit songs that year, "Nadine" and "No Particular Place to Go." He continued to tour but was not so popular. Groups such as The Beatles and The Rolling Stones were the new hits, often singing songs that Chuck had composed. Chuck did not mind; he was glad they were using his music.

By 1970, Chuck was making a music comeback. He recorded two albums, *Back Home Again* and *San Francisco Dues*, which sold well. Then, in 1972, he released "My Ding-A-Ling" which sold more than two million copies. In 1973, Chuck appeared in the movie *Let the Good Times Roll*, a documentary about famous rock-and-roll musicians. He also appeared on television, performing on "American Bandstand's Twenty-fifth Anniversary."

In 1986, Rolling Stones guitarist Keith Richards organized a sixtieth birthday party for Chuck. It featured the most famous singers of rock-and-roll performing Chuck's greatest hits.

Today Chuck is recognized as the most important person in the development of rock and roll and is known as "the creator of rock and roll."

Accomplishments

1955 Signed with Chess Records; released "Maybelline."	**1958** Released "Johnny B. Goode."
	1964 Released *Chuck Berry's Greatest Hits.*
1956 Released "Roll Over Beethoven," "Brown-Eyed Handsome Man," and "Too Much Monkey Business"; appeared in the movie *Rock, Rock, Rock.*	**1972** Released "My Ding-A-Ling."
	1979 Released *Rock It.*
	1980 Released *Rock! Rock! Rock 'n' Roll!*

Natalie Cole

Even as a child, Natalie loved music, and her favorite was rock and roll.

Natalie is the daughter of the famous singer Nat King Cole. Even as a child, Natalie loved music, and her favorite was rock and roll. Although Nat preferred jazz, he would buy Natalie recordings of The Beatles and other rock groups. Sometimes he would sneak in a record of one of the great female jazz musicians such as Ella Fitzgerald and Sarah Vaughan.

When Natalie was eleven, her father bought her a tape recorder. She recorded herself singing and included one of Ella Fitzgerald's greatest hits. When she played the songs for Nat, he told her that she had the talent to become a professional singer.

Natalie formed a jazz trio called the Malibu Music Men, but she wanted to become a doctor and had no interest in a musical career. Nat died in 1965, when Natalie was fifteen. Her mother married again, and the family moved from Los Angeles to Massachusetts.

Natalie attended the University of Massachusetts, and during the summer, she sang at local bars with a band called Black Magic. After she graduated in 1972, she decided to become a singer. She sang at many small night clubs and made her New York debut in 1973. Her audiences wanted her to sing her father's hits, but Natalie wanted to be famous for her own songs and did not want to be known as Nat's daughter. At one point, she even considered changing her name. Soon she developed her own style which combined gospel music and rhythm and blues.

Personality Profile

Career: Singer.

Born: February 6, 1950, in Los Angeles, California, to Nat and Maria Cole.

Education: B.A., University of Massachusetts, 1972.

Awards: Two Grammy awards, 1976; Grammy award, 1977; Image Awards, NAACP, 1976, 1977; American Music Award, 1978; three Grammy awards, 1992.

When Natalie was twenty-four, she auditioned for Chuck Jackson and Marvin Yancy, two songwriters and record producers in Chicago, Illinois. It was the turning point in her career. They wrote songs that fitted her style, and soon she signed a contract with Capitol Records. In 1975, Natalie released her first album, *Inseparable*. The album sold well, and Natalie won two Grammy awards. She also made her first tour.

In 1976, Natalie released the album *Natalie*. She followed this with several other successful albums and television appearances. She was becoming one of the most popular black singers in the United States.

But Natalie found it hard to deal with fame, and she became dependent upon drugs and alcohol. Music reviewers began to criticize her albums, her songs were no longer big sellers, and audiences began to stay away from her performances. In 1983, Natalie started drug rehabilitation therapy. At one point, Natalie's mother had to take control of her affairs. When Natalie was released from the clinic several months later, she was free of drugs.

Since then, Natalie has made a comeback. In 1987, she released her album *Everlasting* which had three hit singles. She followed it with the successful *Good to Be Back* in 1989.

Natalie's most successful album was released when she was forty-one. Entitled *Unforgettable,* it contained twenty-two songs that were made famous by Natalie's father. It had taken her fifteen years to feel comfortable singing Nat's music. In the song "Unforgettable" Natalie's voice is blended with her father's recorded voice. It sounds as if they are singing together. The album has sold more than two million copies.

Accomplishments

1975	Released *Inseparable.*	**1983**	Released *I'm Ready.*
1977	Released *Thankful.*	**1987**	Released *Everlasting.*
1978	Released *Natalie Live.*	**1991**	Released *Unforgettable.*
1979	Released *We're the Best of Friends.*	**1993**	Released *Take a Look.*

Thomas Dorsey

T homas was born in 1899, the son of a Baptist minister in Villa Rica, Georgia. He learned to play the piano at an early age and fell in love with blues music. By the time he was twelve, Thomas had adopted the stage name "Georgia Tom" and was singing and playing in night clubs. He often worked with famous blues singer Ma Rainey.

By 1931, Thomas had composed over 200 blues songs. But Thomas wanted to write church music. He began writing his own hymns using blues and ragtime rhythms. He called his new style "gospel music."

Thomas wrote his first gospel song, "If You See My Savior, Tell Him That You Saw Me," at age twenty-seven after a serious illness. He published the song himself and sent copies to several black churches. Most church members enjoyed the music, but the ministers disliked it. They did not think it was right to play this kind of music in church. But in time, gospel music caught on and within ten years had replaced spiritual music in most black churches. "If You See My Savior" has been translated into fifty languages.

Thomas promoted his new gospel songs through Dorsey Music, a songwriting and publishing company. He performed his first gospel songs in church halls and city streets and played wherever he could get an audience. Some of his most popular songs were "Jesus Is the Light of the World," "How about You," and "Angels Watching over Me." Some of Thomas's songs were later made popular by rock star Elvis Presley and gave rise to a new form of music called soul. By the time Thomas died, he had written about 1,000 gospel songs and about 2,000 blues songs.

One of the most famous singers of Thomas's songs was Mahalia Jackson. She introduced his songs to new audiences around the world and became known as the "Queen of Gospel."

Personality Profile

Career: Gospel music composer and singer.

Born: July 1, 1899, in Villa Rica, Georgia.

Died: January 28, 1993, in Chicago, Illinois.

Education: Chicago Music College.

Awards: Elected to the Georgia Music Hall of Fame and the Nashville Gospel Music Association; National Academy of Recording Arts & Sciences (Grammy) National Trustee Award, 1992.

Thomas's most moving and successful song was "Take My Hand, Precious Lord." He wrote it in 1931, after his wife died during childbirth and their baby died a year later. The song was sung at the funeral of civil rights leader Dr. Martin Luther King, Jr.

In 1983, Thomas's work was featured in the film *Say Amen, Somebody*. The film tells the story of gospel music and features many interviews with Thomas. In 1992, the National Academy of Recording Arts & Sciences presented Thomas with a Grammy award. He is frequently referred to as the grandfather of gospel music.

Thomas died of Alzheimer's disease at age ninety-three. After his death, a group of fans asked the Villa Rica City Council to approve a project that would set up an historic marker at the site of Thomas's birthplace. The project was approved, and signs were placed on the interstate highway to inform travelers that Villa Rica was Thomas Dorsey's home town.

Accomplishments

1926 Wrote first gospel hit, "If You See My Savior, Tell Him That You Saw Me."	**1983** Appeared in the documentary film *Say Amen, Somebody*.
1931 Wrote his best-selling hit, "Take My Hand, Precious Lord."	**1992** Received Grammy award.
1932 Organized the first National Convention of Gospel Choirs and Choruses.	

Whitney Houston

W hitney was born in 1963 into a musical household. Her mother, Cissy, was the choir director at a Baptist church in Newark, New Jersey. She was also a back-up for such famous singers as Aretha Franklin and Elvis Presley. As a child, Whitney watched many of their recording sessions and became friends with Aretha who often visited the Houston home. Whitney wanted to be just like Aretha.

When she was nine, Whitney joined her mother's church choir. During high school, she performed with her mother in night clubs and sang back-up for several musicians in recording studios. Whitney also began a career as a fashion model, appearing in magazines such as *Vogue, Seventeen,* and *Cosmopolitan.*

When she was fifteen, Whitney was offered a contract as a solo singer. But Whitney's parents wanted her to finish school first, so she turned down the offer.

After graduating from high school, Whitney signed with Tara Productions, a company that finds jobs for entertainers. Tara found Whitney new modeling jobs, and she was featured in fashion magazines such as *Essence* and *Harper's Bazaar.* Tara also began to promote her as a singer, and Whitney sang in television commercials and on the albums of other singers and musicians. In 1983, when Whitney sang "Eternal Love" on the album *Paul Jabara and Friends*, music producers began to notice her.

Whitney was the featured singer at a night club in Manhattan, New York, and Tara Productions invited many recording executives and journalists to hear her. One of them was Clive Davis, the president of Arista Records. He was so impressed with Whitney that he offered her a contract.

Clive wanted to make sure Whitney's first album was a success. He had to make sure people knew who she was before her album was released. Clive spent two years and $250,000 promoting Whitney. She appeared on television and was the featured performer in night clubs. Clive lined up the best team of producers and songwriters to work on the album. *Whitney Houston* was finally released in 1985. It was a huge success, and Whitney went on her first national tour which ended with a sell-out performance at Carnegie Hall in New York.

Personality Profile

Career: Singer and actress.

Born: August 9, 1963, in Newark, New Jersey, to John and Cissy Houston.

Education: Mount St. Dominic Academy.

Awards: Numerous Grammy, American Music, and National Music awards; Key to the City of Newark; and MTV's Top Female Pop Vocalist, 1986; American Music Award of Merit, 1994.

In 1986, Whitney sang her hit "The Greatest Love of All" before a nationwide television audience to celebrate the hundreth anniversary of the Statue of Liberty. The next year, she released her second album, *Whitney*, which was followed by *I'm Your Baby Tonight*. In 1993, she starred and sang in the movie *The Bodyguard*, a film about a talented singer who is being stalked by a crazed fan. The songs that Whitney sang for the film made her even more famous. The single "I Will Always Love You" was at the top of the charts for fourteen weeks – longer than any other song in musical history. The song sold five million copies and won Whitney two American Music Awards.

So far, Whitney has had ten Number One singles, outdoing even The Beatles. In 1992, Whitney married singer Bobby Brown. The following year, the couple had a daughter, Bobbi Kristina. The family lives in a mansion in the New Jersey countryside.

Accomplishments

1985	Released *Whitney Houston*; went on first national tour.
1987	Released *Whitney*.
1990	Released *I'm Your Baby Tonight*.
1993	Starred in *The Bodyguard* and released *The Bodyguard* album.

Janet Jackson

In 1973, when she was seven, Janet was performing with her brothers in Las Vegas hotels and night clubs.

Janet's childhood was different from most people's. Her five brothers formed a band called the Jackson Five which her father, Joseph, managed. In 1973, when she was seven, Janet was performing with her brothers in Las Vegas hotels and night clubs. She appeared in "The Jacksons," a summer television variety show.

When Janet was ten, television producer Norman Lear saw her on the show, and he gave her a role in the television comedy "Good Times." Janet played Penny Gordon, an abused child. In 1979, Janet starred in "A New Kind of Family." The show did not last long, but Janet's next role on the popular "Diff'rent Strokes" ran for several years.

Janet's acting and singing kept her so busy that she did not have many friends. Many of her classmates were scared of her because she was famous.

After high school, Janet appeared in the television show "Fame." She played a music major at an arts school. Janet had to dance on the show, and she enjoyed it very much. She decided dance would be a part of her music.

When Janet's father suggested she become a professional singer, she agreed. Still in her teens, she released two albums with the help of her brothers. Both were poorly received.

When she was eighteen, in 1984, Janet eloped with James DeBarge, a member of another singing family and a friend of hers since she was ten. The marriage lasted less than a year.

Personality Profile

Career: Singer, dancer, songwriter, and actress.

Born: May 16, 1966, in Gary, Indiana, to Joseph and Katherine Jackson.

Awards: Two American Music Awards, 1987; American Music Award, 1988; MTV's 1990 Video Vanguard Award; Grammy award, 1990; three American Music Awards, 1991; Best R&B-urban-contemporary video, Soul Train Music Awards, 1991; Humanitarian of the Year Award, Starlight Foundation, 1991.

Janet worked hard for her next album. She went on a diet and took voice and dance lessons for three months. She released *Control* in 1986. Featuring the hit single "What Have You Done for Me Lately?" the album was a huge hit and sold more than eight million copies. Janet's music videos for the album were also popular.

In 1989, Janet produced another best-selling album, *Janet Jackson's Rhythm Nation 1814*. It featured the hits "Miss You Much" and "Escapade." She received many music and video awards and signed a forty-million-dollar, three-album contract with a new recording company, Virgin Records. At that time, it was the highest-paying recording contract in history.

After the sucess of *Rhythm Nation*, Janet went on an international tour. Tickets for her concerts were sold out less than an hour after going on sale. Her show included a two-million-dollar, five-storey set, six dancers, two backup singers, and a seven-piece band. She even had fireworks and a caged panther.

Janet has been called a team player. She enjoys working with other people, and she listens to their comments before making a decision. Music reviewers say she is good at picking talented people with whom she can work.

Janet also donates to charities and education programs. She gives to the United Negro College Fund and supports Cities in Schools, a program in Washington, D.C., which helps young people stay in school. Janet also gives to the Make-a-Wish program which helps dying children.

Accomplishments

1973 Appeared as a singer at Las Vegas night clubs.

1976 Appeared in "The Jacksons" television show.

1977 Appeared in "Good Times."

1979 Appeared in "A New Kind of Family" and "Diff'rent Strokes."

1982 Released first album, *Janet Jackson*.

1984 Released *Dream Street*.

1986 Released *Control*.

1989 Released *Janet Jackson's Rhythm Nation 1814*.

Charley Pride

C harley's parents were farmers, and from the age of five, Charley worked in the cotton fields with his ten brothers and sisters. In the evenings, Charley loved to listen to the radio, especially country-and-western songs. He fell in love with this music, learning the words and singing along with his favorite stars. Later he bought a guitar and taught himself how to play country-and-western music.

At first, Charley wanted to be a baseball player because he felt it would be a way of escaping the cotton fields. He decided that after he was a famous ball player, he would try and become a singer. Charley joined several baseball teams, and he was a good player, but he never made the major leagues.

Charley went to Helena, Montana, in 1960, when he was twenty-two, and got a job working in a tin-smelting factory. A country-music group lived next door, and they asked Charley to join them as a guitarist and singer.

Charley played in night clubs around the city and also played baseball in the evenings. One night he played baseball and sang for the crowd. The next day, a newspaper ran a feature article about the singing baseball player.

In 1963, Charley met Red Sovine, a famous country-and-western singer. Red told him to go to Nashville, Tennessee, where most country singers went to find a recording studio. The next year, after realizing that he would never be a professional baseball player, Charley took his advice. In Nashville he met Jack Johnson, a record producer who gave Charley a contract and asked him to record seven songs. "Snakes Crawl at Night," Charley's first hit single, was one of these songs.

At that time, there were no successful African-American country singers. The managers of Charley's record company did not want to tell the public Charley was black because they were afraid white listeners would not buy his music. Charley's first three albums did not have a photo of him. One night in 1966, at a concert in Detroit, 10,000 people loudly applauded when Charley was announced, but they quickly stopped when he stepped on stage. After the first shock was over and Charley sang a few songs, the crowd began to cheer for him again. They did not care if he was black or white, they just loved his music.

Personality Profile

Career: Singer and businessman.

Born: March 18, 1938, in Sledge, Mississippi, to Mack Pride, Sr.

Education: Sledge Junior High School.

Awards: Most Promising Male Artist, several country music publications, 1966; Trendsetter Award, *Billboard*, 1970; Entertainer of the Year, Music Operators of America, 1971; Grammy awards, 1971, 1972; Best Male Vocalist Award, Country Music Association; Favorite Male Vocalist in Country Music, American Music Awards, 1976.

Over the years, Charley continued to produce best-selling hits. He recorded more than forty albums, and his music is popular in many countries, especially Australia. Charley appeared on several television shows including "The Lawrence Welk Show," "Hee Haw," and "The Johnny Cash Show." He has also won numerous awards for his music.

Throughout his career, people have asked Charley why he sings country music, a field dominated by white singers. Charley always answers that he just sings in a way that is natural to him, and that he is pleased to be the first African-American country-music star. He hopes his success will convince other black musicians to consider a career in country music.

Charley is also a successful business executive. He is a director of a Texan bank, a partner in three music publishing houses, and the owner of an outdoor-grill manufacturing company. Charley's love of baseball remains strong, and his dream is one day to own a baseball team.

Accomplishments

1965 Released first single, "Snakes Crawl at Night."

1967 Released first album, *Country Charley Pride.* Appeared at the Grand Ole Opry in Nashville, Tennessee.

1970 First million-record seller, "Kiss an Angel Good Morning."

1971 Released Grammy award-winning album *Did You Think to Pray.*

1973 Released hit single "Amazing Love."

1974 Released hit single "We Could."

1988 Released hit single "Shouldn't It Be Easier than This."

1989 Released hit single "Amy's Eyes."

Index

3 4 5 6 7 8 9 0 Printed in the United States 4 3 2 1